How We Use

Plastic

Chris Oxlade

www.raintreepublishers.co.uk

Visit our website to find out more information about **Raintree** books.

To order:

 ☎ Phone 44 (0) 1865 888112

📄 Send a fax to 44 (0) 1865 314091

💻 Visit the Raintree bookshop at **www.raintreepublishers.co.uk** to browse our catalogue and order online.

First published in Great Britain by Raintree,
Halley Court, Jordan Hill, Oxford OX2 8EJ,
part of Harcourt Education.
Raintree is a registered trademark of Harcourt
Education Ltd.

Editorial: Nick Hunter
Design: Kim Saar
Picture Research: Heather Sabel and Amor
    Montes de Oca
Production: Alex Lazarus

Originated by Ambassador Litho Ltd.
Printed and bound in China by South China
Printing Company

ISBN 1 844 43266 1
08 07 06 05 04
10 9 8 7 6 5 4 3 2 1

British Library Cataloguing in Publication Data
Oxlade, Chris
How We Use Plastic. - (Using Materials)
620.1'923
A full catalogue record for this book is available from
the British Library.

Acknowledgements
The publishers would like to thank the following for
permission to reproduce photographs:
Corbis pp. **6**, **8** (Pablo Corral), **9** (Vo Trung
Dung/SYGMA), **17**, **19** (CB Productions), **21**, **25**, **28**
(J. A. Giordano/SABA); Dwight Kuhn p. **15**; Getty
Images pp. **7** (Stone), **26** (The Image Bank); Harcourt
Education pp. **4** (Robert Lifson), **11**, **29** (Greg
Williams); Jonah Calinawan p. **16**; Meonshore Studios
Ltd (Mike French) pp. **18**, **22**; Peter Kubal pp. **13**, **20**;
Science Photo Library pp. **14**, **27** (Maximillian Stock
Ltd); Tom Pantages p. **23**; Visuals Unlimited pp. **5**
(Mark S. Skalny), **24** (Jeff J. Daly); Yves Tzaud pp.
10, **12**.

Cover photographs reproduced with permission of
Corbis (top) and Getty Images (Howard Kingsnorth)
(bottom).

Every effort has been made to contact copyright
holders of any material reproduced in this book.
Any omissions will be rectified in subsequent printings
if notice is given to the publishers.

The paper used to print this book comes from
sustainable resources.

Contents

Any words appearing in bold, **like this**, are explained in the Glossary.

Plastic and its properties

All the things we use at home, school and work are made from materials. Plastic is a material. We use plastics for many different jobs. You can see plastics almost everywhere you look. We use them to make bags, boxes, packaging, clothes, toys and thousands of parts for machines.

All the parts of this toy are made of plastic.

These plastic drinking straws are made from soft, bendy plastic.

Properties tell us what a material is like. There are many different sorts of plastic. Each one has its own properties. Some plastics are very hard and strong. Others are soft and easy to bend. Some plastics go soft when they are heated up. Other plastics stay hard. All plastics are light and last a long time.

Don't use it!
*The different properties of materials make them useful for different jobs. These properties can also make them unsuitable for some jobs. For example, most plastics **melt** when they get very hot. So we cannot use plastic to make ovens.*

Where does plastic come from?

Plastics are not **natural** materials. They are **artificial** materials made in factories. Plastics are made from **chemicals**. We get the chemicals from natural materials such as crude oil, gas and coal. These are called fossil fuels. Fossil fuels are fuels that have formed over millions of years from the remains of dead plants and animals. Sometimes we get chemicals for plastics from rocks or plants such as cotton.

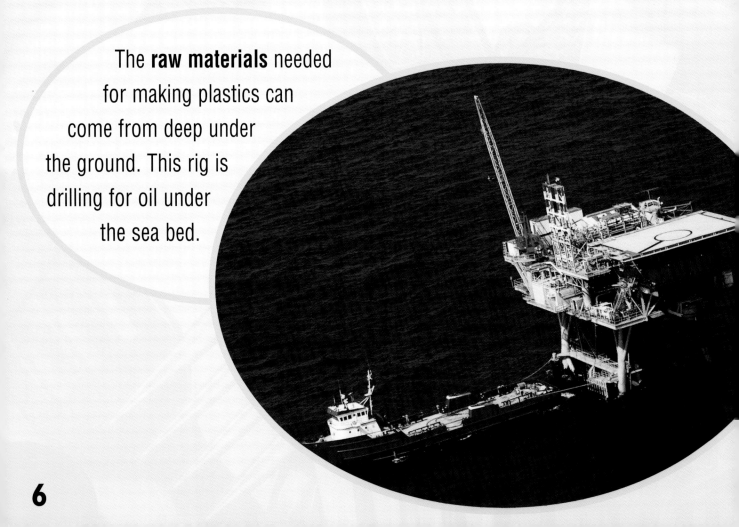

The **raw materials** needed for making plastics can come from deep under the ground. This rig is drilling for oil under the sea bed.

This is what a strip of film looks like under a **microscope**. This film is made from plastic.

Crude oil, gas and coal are split up into many chemicals. Then the chemicals can be used to make different sorts of plastics. Most plastics come out of the factory in chips and **granules**, ready to be made into things.

The first plastic

The first plastic was made over 100 years ago. It was called celluloid because it was made from a chemical called cellulose. It was used to make film for cameras. We get cellulose from wood. Celluloid has been replaced by modern plastics with more useful ***properties***.

Plastic parts

Plastic is easy to make into objects of many different sizes and shapes. We use it to make things, from tiny parts of machines to whole tables and chairs. Plastic parts are tough and long-lasting. They are also cheap to make. Small things, such as plastic cups and spoons, are so cheap that we can use them once and throw them away. We say that they are **disposable**.

Plastic is a good material for things we use outdoors. Plastic does not **rot** like wood, or **rust** like metal.

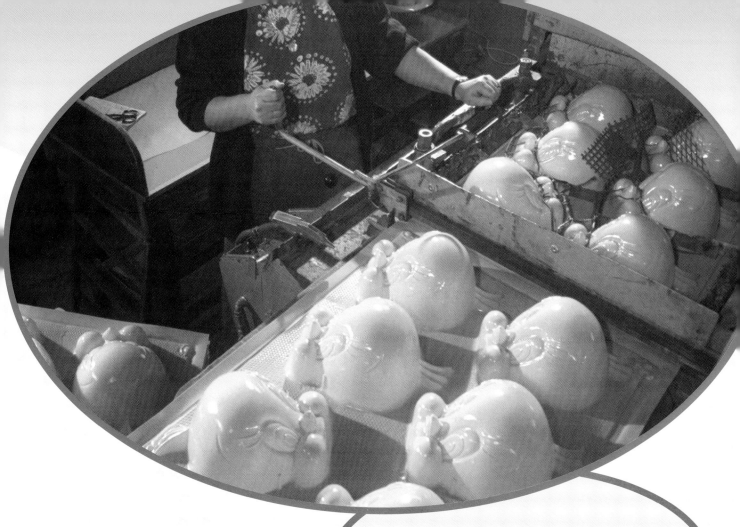

> By using moulds, we can make lots of plastic objects that are exactly the same.

Moulding parts

Plastic parts are made in **moulds**. A mould is a block of metal with a space inside. The space is the shape of the object that is going to be made. Plastic is heated until it **melts** and then poured into the mould. When the plastic has cooled down again, and hardened, the mould is opened and the part is taken out. Every plastic part made in a mould is exactly the same shape.

9

Plastic containers

Many plastics do not let water or air flow through them. They are **waterproof** and **airtight**. These **properties** make plastics good materials for containers. We make fizzy drink bottles, sandwich boxes, storage boxes, rubbish bins, bowls and buckets from plastic. Some special plastic food containers can be put in an oven without **melting**.

Fizzy drink bottles are made from a strong plastic called polyethylene terephthalate (PET for short).

These plastic containers are used with takeaway meals, to keep sauces warm.

Plastic instead of glass

Many containers, such as bottles and drinking glasses, are made from glass. Glass is a **brittle** material. Glass containers break easily if they are dropped. Plastic can bend without snapping. So plastic containers do not break if they are dropped. We use plastic for containers that might get dropped, such as drinking bottles for babies.

Don't use it!

*Most plastics are affected by **chemicals**. For example, some **acids** can eat away plastic. When we cannot store chemicals such as acid in plastic containers, we have to use glass containers instead.*

Plastics in buildings

Builders use plastics when they build houses and other buildings. Window frames, door frames and gutters are often made of plastic. So are pipes that carry away rainwater, and pipes that carry away waste water from baths, showers and toilets. All these things are made from a plastic called polyvinyl chloride (PVC for short).

The parts of this window frame were joined by heating their ends to make them stick together.

Plastic pipes will last hundreds of years.

We sometimes use plastic instead of wood for window frames because plastic does not **rot** like wood. Some people prefer wood though because it looks more **natural** than plastic. We do not need to put **preservatives** or paint on plastic. We use plastic instead of metal for pipes because plastic does not **rust** like metal.

Don't use it!

Some plastics are strong, but they are not strong enough to hold up a building. So we cannot use plastics for the main part of a house, such as the walls and the roof. We need to use very strong materials such as brick, steel and concrete instead.

Plastic fibres and fabrics

A **fibre** is a thin strand of material. The hairs on your head are fibres. Plastic fibres are stronger than **natural** fibres such as cotton and wool. Plastic fibres are made by pushing hot, soft plastic through tiny holes. The most common plastic fibres are called polyester, acrylic and polypropylene.

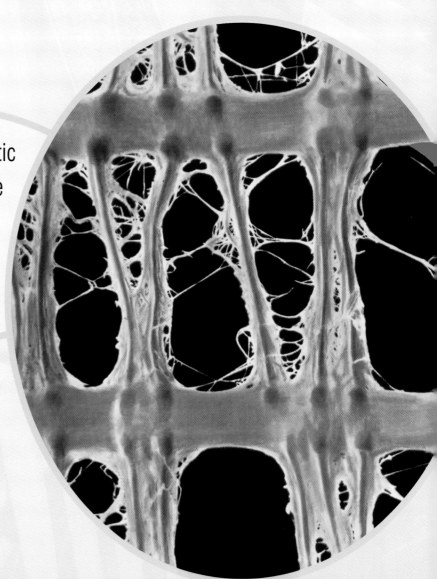

This is what plastic netting looks like through a **microscope**. You can see the fibres twisted together.

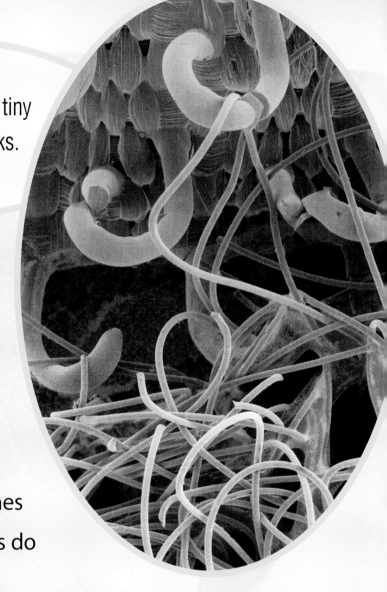

Velcro is made from tiny plastic loops and hooks.

Polyester fibres and acrylic fibres are woven together to make **fabrics**. Polyester fabrics are made into clothes such as shirts and waterproof jackets. Clothes made from acrylic fabrics do not get creases in them.

Waterproof fabrics

Some fabrics are made from sheets of plastic. For example, chairs are sometimes covered with sheets of PVC fabric. The fabric often has a pattern on it to make it look like leather. We also put PVC on woven fabrics to make them **waterproof**.

Plastics for protection

Some sorts of plastic are extremely tough. They bend a little bit, but they are very hard to break. We use tough plastics to make containers for delicate equipment. For example, computers, mobile telephones and radios have hard cases made from a tough plastic called ABS. If you drop them accidentally the plastic doesn't usually break.

The lenses in these sunglasses are made from tough polycarbonate. They should not break or scratch.

The plastic used to make this safety helmet is very tough.

We make safety equipment from tough plastics, too. For example, safety goggles are made of acrylic. They do not shatter into pieces if something hits them. Safety helmets for people on building sites or mountain climbers are made from ABS plastic or a plastic called polycarbonate. They protect people's heads from falling objects.

Plastics, heat and electricity

Heat cannot flow through plastics very well. If you put a plastic spoon in a hot drink the spoon's handle stays cool. Only the part of the spoon that touches the hot drink will heat up. We often use plastic for pan handles because the plastic stays cool when the pan is hot. We say that plastic does not **conduct** heat well.

This plastic spoon went soft when it was put in hot water.

The electronic parts inside machines are joined to a kind of plastic that does not melt if it gets hot.

Most plastics go soft when they get hot. Scientists call these plastics thermoplastics. When thermoplastics cool down they go hard again. Some plastics do not go soft when they get hot. Scientists call these plastics thermosetting plastics. We use thermosetting plastics to make things that might get hot. For example, electric plugs and sockets are made of thermosetting plastics.

Electricity cannot flow through plastics either. We cover metal wires that carry electricity with plastic called PVC. The plastic stops electricity jumping from one wire to another by accident.

Plastics for packaging

Some plastics are very light. This is because they are full of millions of tiny air bubbles. Filling a piece of plastic with bubbles makes it expand so it is bigger. We call these sorts of plastic expanded plastic or foamed plastic.

The most common expanded plastic is called expanded polystyrene. It is the white plastic that is used to protect things, such as televisions, inside their packing boxes.

This is what expanded polystyrene looks like under a **microscope**. You can see the tiny bubbles inside.

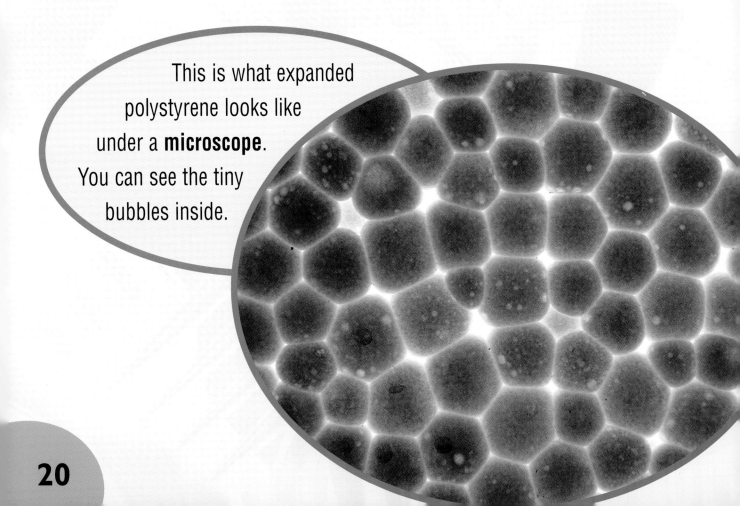

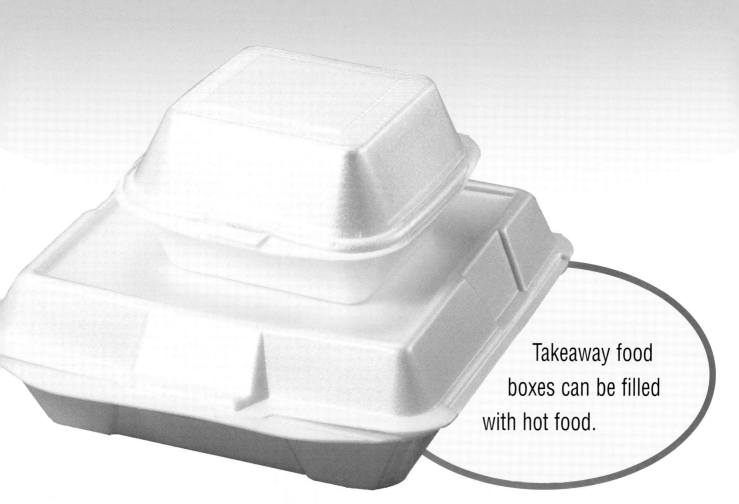

Takeaway food boxes can be filled with hot food.

Insulating

We also use expanded plastic for food containers. Hot drinks, burgers and chips often come in boxes made from expanded plastic. The tiny bubbles inside the plastic stop heat escaping. They **insulate** the food. This keeps the food warm and stops your fingers getting too hot!

Don't use it!

Many cushions and mattresses are made from expanded plastic called polyurethane foam. It is soft, bendy and light. This plastic is also inflammable, meaning it burns very easily, so we cannot use this sort of plastic where it might catch fire.

Squashy plastics

Some types of plastic are rubbery. You can squash or stretch things made from rubbery plastics. They always go back into shape afterwards. The material we call rubber was once made only from **natural** rubber, which comes from trees. Today it is usually made from rubbery plastic or a mixture of natural rubber and plastic. There is not enough natural rubber for all the rubber we need.

Some toys are made specially to be squeezed.

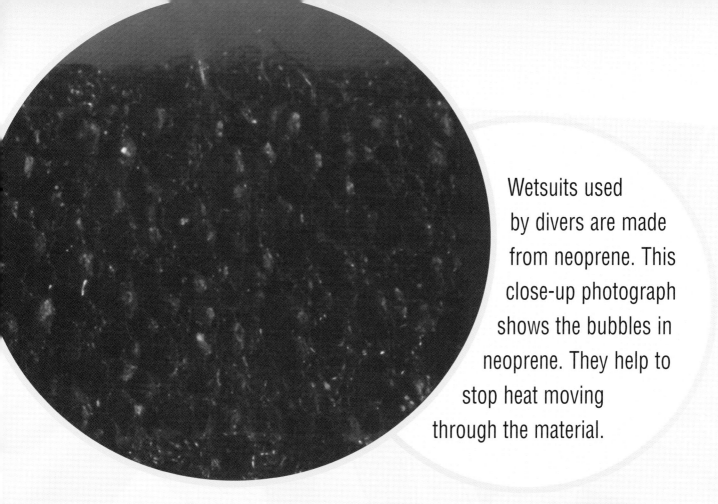

Wetsuits used by divers are made from neoprene. This close-up photograph shows the bubbles in neoprene. They help to stop heat moving through the material.

Don't use it!

We cannot use squashy, rubbery plastics in places where we do not want them to stretch. For example, we would not use a rubbery plastic to make a fizzy drink bottle. The sides would stretch and the bottle would fall over.

The main use of rubbery plastics is for making tyres for cars, trucks, bikes and buses. The rubbery tyres give passengers a smooth ride over bumps in the road. Tyres also grip the road to stop wheels sliding. We also use rubbery plastics to make soft soles for shoes and boots.

Plastic sheets

Plastic sheets are light, bendy, **waterproof** and **airtight**. We make plastic sheets into many different products. Millions of plastic bags are made from sheets of a plastic called polyethylene. They are light, strong, waterproof and cheap. We use plastic bags for hundreds of jobs such as carrying shopping, for storing food and collecting rubbish.

Bubble-wrap is made from two sheets of plastic glued together with air bubbles trapped between them.

Sweet wrappers are made from small pieces of plastic sheet.

We make plastic bags by blowing air into hot, liquid plastic. This blows the plastic up into a huge, long tube. When the plastic cools down it is cut into short tubes. One end of a short tube is heated up to join the sides together and make a bag.

We also make plastic sheets to wrap food and sweets, for shower curtains, for drinks containers and to cover things to protect them from water and dirt.

High-tech plastics

Scientists are **inventing** new plastics with special **properties** all the time. They might be very hard, very strong, very light or stay hard when they get very hot. For example, a plastic called PTFE has a very slippery surface. It is also tough and does not **melt** even when it gets very hot. These properties make it good for non-stick pans.

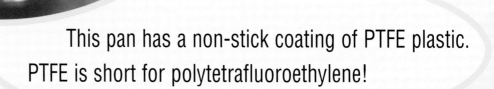

This pan has a non-stick coating of PTFE plastic. PTFE is short for polytetrafluoroethylene!

This special liquid is used to hold the different materials in a composite material together.

Plastics and other materials

Some materials are made from plastic mixed with other substances. These materials are called **composites**. A composite material has the properties of both materials. For example, a material called glass-reinforced plastic (GRP for short) is made up of plastic mixed with thin glass **fibres**. The glass fibres make the GRP very strong.

Plastic and the environment

Plastics do not **rot** or **rust**. This means that plastic objects such as rain gutters last a long time. It also means that plastic rubbish will not rot away either. When we throw plastics away we also waste the **chemicals** that the plastics were made from. Most of the chemicals come from oil and if we keep using up oil it will eventually run out because we cannot replace it.

When we throw away plastic things they last for hundreds of years in the environment.

Recycling bins are provided in most areas, making recycling very easy.

Recycling plastics

We can help the environment by using plastics again instead of throwing them away. This is called recycling. It also saves using up precious oil. Some sorts of plastic can be **melted** to make new plastic.

Find out for yourself

The best way to find out more about plastics is to investigate plastics for yourself. Look around your home and school for plastics. Think about why plastic was used for each job. What **properties** make it the right material for the job? You will find the answers to many of your questions in this book. You can also look in other books and on the Internet.

Books to read

Science Answers: Grouping Materials, Carol Ballard (Heinemann Library, 2003)

Discovering Science: Matter, Rebecca Hunter (Raintree, 2003)

Science Files: Plastics, Steve Parker (Heinemann Library, 2002)

Using the Internet

Try searching the Internet to find out about things to do with plastics. Websites can change, so if one of the links below no longer works, don't worry. Use a search engine, such as www.yahooligans.com or www.internet4kids.com. For example, you could try searching using the keywords 'thermoplastic, 'polycarbonate' and 'plastic bottles'.

Websites

A great site, which explains all about different materials:
http://www.bbc.co.uk/schools/revisewise/science/materials/

A fun site that explains how plastic is made and used:
www.psrc.usm.edu/macrog/floor1.htm

Disclaimer

All the Internet addresses (URLs) given in this book were valid at the time of going to press. However, due to the dynamic nature of the Internet, some addresses may have changed, or sites may have ceased to exist since publication. While the author and publishers regret any inconvenience this may cause readers, no responsibility for any such changes can be accepted by either the author or the publishers.

Glossary

acid liquid that can eat away at materials

airtight describes a material that does not let air pass through it

artificial describes a material that is not found naturally. It is made by people.

brittle describes a material that snaps easily

chemical substance that we use to make other substances, or for jobs such as cleaning

composite material made from two other materials used together. For example, glass-reinforced plastic is made from glass and plastic.

conduct let heat or electricity pass through

disposable describes an object that is meant to be thrown away after it is used

electricity form of energy that flows along wires

fabric flat sheet of bendy material, such as cotton or leather

fibre long, thin, bendy piece of material

granule small lump of a material

insulate stop heat escaping

invent make or discover something for the first time

melt turn from a solid into a liquid by heating

microscope instrument used for looking at things in tiny detail. Microscopes make things look much larger.

mould block of metal with a space in the centre. When molten plastic is poured into the mould it sets, making an object the same shape as the inside of the mould.

natural describes anything that is not made by people

preservative chemical that helps to stop a material rotting

property quality of a material that tell us what it is like. Hard, soft, bendy and strong are all properties.

raw material natural material that is used to make other materials

rot to break down

rust process that makes iron and steel weak and crumbly. It happens when iron or steel is left in damp air.

waterproof describes a material that does not let water pass through it

Index

Titles in the *Using Materials* series include:

Hardback   1 844 43260 2

Hardback   1 844 43267 X

Hardback   1 844 43265 3

Hardback   1 844 43263 7

Hardback   1 844 43266 1

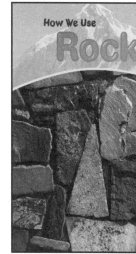

Hardback   1 844 43261 0

Hardback   1 844 43262 9

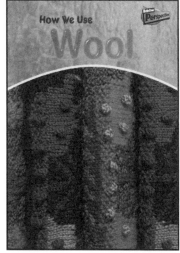

Hardback   1 844 43268 8

Find out about the other titles in this series on our website www.raintreepublishers.co.uk